T0070152

W.A.G.A.

Author
Samuel Patrino

authorHOUSE®

AuthorHouse™
1663 Liberty Drive
Bloomington, IN 47403
www.authorhouse.com
Phone: 833-262-8899

Published by AuthorHouse 07/29/2022

ISBN: 978-1-6655-6523-3 (sc)
ISBN: 978-1-6655-6522-6 (e)

Library of Congress Control Number: 2022913232

Print information available on the last page.

Dedicated to the original W.A.G.A. foursome
that started playing together in the 1980's

PROLOGUE

Through the years, I have met many interesting people on the golf course. There are always many golf stories being told from those you meet. Whether they were true or made up. It's fun to hear. I thought writing them down just to have them and publish them so everyone could hear them.

So through the years I wrote some of events down that I witness while playing golf with a group that met twice a week starting last March thru November and sometimes into December. We played in all kinds of weather. It's amazing how far the ball travels on frozen ground.

I thought many times that I should publish a book with these many stories. Then, why would anyone want to read these stories.

But then I said to myself why not.

Many of the golfers that these little events are about

are longer with us. They are playing up in the clouds and having a good time.

Most of these little stories are as true as I can remember. Maybe added a few little words to make a point.

Arnold Palmer had a great tip for all golfers, "How to take five strokes off anyone's game. It's called an ERASER."

Contents

Thru the years I have met many interesting people on the golf course. There are always many golf stories being told from those you meet. Whether they were true or made up. Its fun to hear. I thought writing them down just to have them and publish them so every one could hear them.

So thru the years I wrote some of events down that I witness while playing golf with a group that met twice a week starting last March thru November and sometimes into December. We played in all kinds of weather. Its amazing how far the ball travels on frozen ground.

I thought many times that I should publish a book with these many stories. Then, why would anyone want to read these stories.

But, then I said to my self why not.

Many of the golfers that these little events are about are longer with us. They are playing up in the clouds and having a good time.

Most of these little stories are as true as I can remember. Maybe added a few Little words to make a point.

Arnold Palmer had a great tip for all golfers "How to take five strokes off anyones game.

Its call an ERASER"

READ ON.

There are so many things we all want out of life. When you have arrived at the point of leaving the work force and want some thing to do and enjoy doing it with no one looking over your shoulder. The one item is to play golf, right? Well, it may be enjoyable and yet taxing. This is a short and fairly accurate account of a group of guys who found life after the grind of work doing something a few days a week and enjoying being with others on the golf course hitting and chasing a little white ball for four to five hours.

Now anyone in their right mind would wonder if these few needed some mental care. Many times you would find them walking the course in all kinds of weather. You heard the saying thru rain, snow and hail the Mail will go thru. So the same is true of most of the W.A.G.A. group as they love the game and will play at it until they are ready to go under the grass. They have played on ice, snow, and rain in freezing temperature.

Chapter
The First Tee

Here we go again. First group up on the tee.

That's the battle cry of some twenty some golfers or more. It's the cry that goes on the same time two days a week, every year on the same golf course for the number of weeks that you can play in the mid-west. It starts some time in April and ends late November or sometime early December if we are lucky. But whatever, the cry of hit the ball. When you are playing well and scoring a lot of points for your team and your teammates are having a good day that could mean you could win some money. But you will not to become rich from the winnings. Not enough to buy groceries for the day. Then there are days you wonder what in the hell I am doing out here. Nothing is going right. But, no matter how bad you played that day, you show up the next golf day for another adventure. It's a rewarding /punishment, so they say.

For some time now I have been thinking of writing about the W.A,G.A. group. This is group of guys come from all walks of life. They come to play golf and have fun and relax on a golf course. If saying a few choice words or thinking of sending your golf club into another world or in the pond, you are with the right group. There are times when it's more work than relaxing. Or some might say that their wife are happier than hell to want them out of the house for a little peace of mind. Whatever.

The W.A.G.A. group started playing golf together some 30 some years ago in a small town northwest of Chicago. The golf course is located in a small suburb right in the middle of town where homes were build after the 2nd World War. If you didn't know the area you won't know that there was a golf course there. It's an interesting course with a lot of trees and some very narrow fairways, small greens and a few sand traps. There are 11 water crossings, but not too long a course and fun to play. Sometimes.

So for the average golfer like the W.A.G.A. golfer it's their kind of course. On a day when nothing seems to be going right, you could easily score over a 100 or more. At least most of us could. Thru the years there were members that would score well in their early years, but some how as they aged so did their score.

This is were just a few retired men who meet every Tuesday and Thursday about 8:30 in the morning for a round of golf. They were basically pretty good golfers in their earlier days. They come from all walks of life-Sales Managers, Bankers, Creative Writers, Advertising Executives, Small Business Owners, Plumbers, Lawyer, Marketing, Real Estate Sales, Barbers, School Teachers, former high school Coaches and CPA's. You named a profession and there is one of playing in the group.

Most of the players have played the course for more than 20 years. They know the course. From their tee shot they know pretty much what club to use for their next shot. They know where not to hit and when to lay up and all those things a golfer should know. But as golfers go, after they hit the ball, the comment you would hear "what a dumb shot" or "why did I hit there". The most famous battle cry : "Oh S___there I go again". Which means I've hit the ball there before and I am doing it again, how dumb can you be. What that meant was, there was a bush in the way or there would be a tree or there was no shot to hit down the fairway or to the green. Of course everyone in the foursome would know what the golfer remarks meant as each one at one time or another have been there and had the same remarks.

I am getting ahead of myself as I really wanted to tell you how it all started. I had just retired and had played golf on this course for some years on the weekend. There were a few golfers that had retired before me that I knew and had been playing during the week.

The first W.A.G.A. group had been playing together for a few years. they were just a fouesome.At the start I was asked to play with them from time to time. After a few weeks I was invited to play with them on a regular bases. Sometimes there would be four golfers, but most of the time, there were enough to have two foursomes. There were not many retired golfers in those days so who ever got to the course first would get a least two tee times. As time went on it seem more retired golfers were coming out of the wood works and it got to a point that we had to start getting more tee times a few days in advance. The group grew to a point that we had to limit the amount that could play in the W.A.G.A. group.

Chapter 2

Membership to the W.A.G.A.

How would you become a member of this elite group? That is a good question. As I said before, the original group was one or two foursome in its early days. As time went on the W.A.G.A. grew. Golfers started to retire like flies. Within the first two years the group had gotten to as many as three to four foursomes. A few years later we would have as many as eight foursomes. It had gotten too big and hard to manage. A vote was taken and a rule was put in that only thirty-two names would be listed as regular members of the W.A.G.A. group. Any other person whose name was not on the regular list could sign in as an alternate. If there was room and we need another golfer the first name on the alternate list could play and so on.

How did we arrive at Thirty two members on the offical list?

Now if and when we had all thirty – two players on a given day and the first group would tee off about 9:00 A.M., the last group would tee off just before 10:00 A.M. That's a long time to hang around before you get to play. (It might sounds like a bunch of old women. How would you like to arrive at a golf course and wait an hour and a half to play a round of golf. So we voted and all agreed and the rule was put in.) But on the back end of the day the first foursome would have to wait around until the last players can in to see if you won. You see there was big money involved. The winning team members could win all of maybe twelve dollars. But it also meant a lot of beer could be consume waiting around.

Now how does a person become a member of this elite group and/or able to put his name on the sign – up sheet as alternate? There are no membership forms to fill out or at least I never saw one. There is no annual membership dues. You didn't need a sponsor to join the group. You didn't have to take Physical or have a letter from a doctor saying that you were fit to play golf. But maybe we should have had a mental test to take to see if you qualify to be part of the group.

This is how you become part of the W.A.G.A. You show up at the golf course and say to the member who was running the golf group that day that if you need a player you were available. If one was needed and no other alternate was around you would be ask to play. Then you can in the future put your name on the alternate list.

You become a regular (if your name is drawn from a hat or there are no other alternates on the waiting list) when one of the original members who may have moved away (we did have a few) or past on to next world.

There have been a few members who have gone on to their next life. They most likely started a W.A.G.A. golf group up there. (I wonder if there are any water crossing way up there)

So with the W.A.G.A. growing some rules had to be put into effect. Like a sign up sheet. One was made up with everyone's name listed and you have to check your name off if you were going to play on the next scheduled play date. So we know how many players should show up to play.

Chapter 3

Off to The Golf Course

As you probably know as a golfer, that after you play with fellow golfers for a few years you get know what they are going to say after every shot. Comments like – there I go again, why did I do that or O –S_____. Those are a few and there many more to come. The original group really were there to enjoy a day out on the golf course. And of course a wager had to be made. If it was only a foursome it would the high and low could win.

Handicap against the other two-middle handicap, low net score. When we had two foursome it would be one team against the other, two best ball with handicap. The big wager was a dollar for each nine holes and a dollar for the total eighteen hole score. That's big money.

Chapter 4

The Sign Up

After a few years, after more of them retired from the work force more wanted to play with the group. It got to a point that it was hard to know who was playing and how many wanted to play in order to get tee times so could play. A sheet was put together listing all those would like to play on Tuesday and Thursday and each individual had to check off after name is they planned to play on each one of those days. Well the names on the sheets grew year after year. From around twelve it grew to twenty and then to thirty-two. The original group had a talk and decided that this should be the limit. And that a shorter list be made up of additional players as alternates who might show up and be picked if any players were needed. Well, there were many stories surrounding this plan. A few will be told in later chapters of this epic. The sheets were located in the Men's locker room and each member had to check their name off if they were planning to play on any given Tuesday or Thursday. There were two columns, one if you were playing and the other if you were not. Not many would take the time to check off the not playing column.

At one point there were as many as eight alternates on the sheet. The rule for the Alternates was that they had to be there before eight a.m. to be considered if any were needed to fill out a foursome or fill out a tee time with foursome. The rule for the regulars was they had to be at the golf course at least a half hour before the first tee time. There were times when the regular was not there on time so an alternate was picked in his place. There would be a few choice words on those rare occasions. But, the rule was made and held to by those in charge of putting the groups together each day. Each year at the annual Xmas Luncheon an election would be held to elect three of the members to be in charge for the coming year. The same guys have been elected year after year. I always wondered why no one else wanted the job. The three have always said if any one complains long and hard enough we would elect him the next year. This one of our saying when someone complained long and hard during the Year. We just would say, "Hey, we are going to elect you to run the show Next year", for some reason that always stop what ever the complained was.

Chapter 5

The Morning Drawings

Every morning the sheet in the Men's locker room is taken down and taken into the coffee room where the individual cards of those who checked their names to play that day were pulled from the famous gray box that contained the cards of all the players and their latest handicap. This is were it really all starts. When zero hour arrives, which is about half hour before our first tee time the cards are put in order according to each ones handicap, the top row is those A player whose handicap is the lowest of the group. Depending how many show up that day, can be 24 to 32(the max) the group would be the lows handicap players. The A-B-C- and D follow. The big moans and groans come every two weeks. This when the new handicaps come out. Oh, nuts I don't get a stroke on 16. Dam I don't get one on 13. This goes on and on. Only those who handicap goes up are in a happy situation. They get more strokes and can get more points for the team. The game that is played most of the time is called two best balls. That is the best net score by two of the players in the foursome on a given hole.

First tee is where many quotes are made. Those quotes are gems Many of us have no idea where the ball was going to end up. But there is a Comment for every ball hit by most of the players. Now I should state that Are a few of the golfers that can hit straight and a good distance? Some of the Sayings after they have hit the ball:

State in the fairway!

Don't go into that bush!

There I go again, right into those damn Trees!

Oh boy I pulled it again!

Bounce right!

Bounce left!

Don't slice

Hook - Hook

Find an opening!

Give a good lie in the rough!

You got a shot there! Yeah, sure, wait to we get there.

I am sure I'll come up with a few more before I finish writing.

Now you have to remember that when you are on the

first tee with 3 other golfers, you are a team. You try to give each other encouragement. Like, Nice swing, even though you wonder how he ever hit the ball. Or nice shot and the ball goes about hundred yards. Your ok and your behind a tree. We try to give other a pat on the back. It's the fun of the game and that was what everyone wanted when this group started playing together.

Chapter 6

Senior Moments

This is one chapter that has to be written as I am sure it happens with every senior group that plays together no matter where. The W.A.G.A. group has a rule that you have to be at the course at least a half-hour before the first tee time. Many abide by this rule. Many would get there early just to talk and have coffee. Mostly about who had won the day before or the weather. So when the teams are draw and the first group should be going up to the starter. It's a rare day that someone in the group had forgotten to get his ticket. When the starter asks for his ticket and he discovers that he didn't get a receipt, back to the pro shop for his ticket. That has happen many times. Thank god we are not on a time schedule. If we were we would be in deep trouble. If we were running a company and had absent minded works forgetting to do things like this we would be broke in no time.

And then there a few rare occasions' situations, which are plain, dumb. How about this one. Twosome drives up in a golf cart to the golf starter and the starter asks what they had planned to do that day. They asked him what he was talking about and the starter points to the back of cart. They turn to discover that there were no golf clubs on the cart. They had taken their golf clubs out of the car and dropped them off in front of the pro stop and checked in and gotten their tickets and cart key. But forgot to put their clubs on the cart. Now this what is called senior moment. There have been times when one would get up on the first tee to discover that he forgot to put his golf shoes on. You wonder how he found the golf course that day. Now you would wonder how a group like this could stay together for many years and have fun playing golf.

There other occasions on the golf course when someone in the group has hard time following their golf ball after they hit. They were sure it was hit real well and it traveled a long distance through the trees only to find out it was hundred yards shorter. As we grow older and lose some of our strength the ball doesn't go as far. It's hard for us to accept this fact. The days when we hit a five iron 160 to 170 yards. Those days have long gone by. Today we would be happy if the ball traveled 120 yards, maybe.

Get on with the game.

We finally get on the first green and are hoping to get a few points. One guys in the trap and one hit his chip shot too hard and is off the back of the green and has to chip back.

We do try to help each other putting. There are a lot of choice words after a putt.

It didn't brake. Oh S—I didn't see that brake. There I go again rimed that damn cup again. Comments from your fellow teammates, like Whoa, slow down. Hit the cup, nice putt, you pull it, hit a brick wall. I can go on and on. You've all been there and have heard more language and comments that could fill a book. After you finish play on the first green the usually saying is, OK we got that out of our systems lets get it going on the next hole.

Chapter 7

Second Hole

It starts all over again. Damn, there I go again into those trees. Or, I didn't hit. I looked up. I don't think there was a phrase ever said on a golf course anywhere in the world that was not said one time or the other by one of the W.A.G.A. members. They are truly average play it again golfer like any one golfer who has ever been on a golf course.

After doing well on the second hole, confidence sets in and you hope your group is about to play well for the rest of the round. Well sometimes the team does well and sometime it doesn't. Our second hole is the number 1 handicap hole of the course. There are very, very few players of our group who can get on the green in two. I haven't seen one in many, many years. Three shot maybe and for most of us four is the likely number. Many of the players get two strokes and to shoot a six with two scores and hold par is a good score for the team. Those that come in with a five and get two stroke on that hole is a hero. If you score a point or two on this hole you are doing great. Holding par is great.

Chapter 8

Each Tee

Each tee or hole has its known set of situation as far as this group is concern. Having played many years on the course each player has had Good and bad results. If there was water or cross or a very narrow fairwayTo hit to a lot go through each of our minds as we get set to hit the ball. Of course we try to cheer each other up hoping to score well and get some points for the team. But no matter what happens we are happy to be able to get out and play a round to of golf.

There some of the golfers in the group that you know will hit the ball right down the fairway and be in good position most of the time. The are some of us that they might say a Hail Mary for and hope that we hit the ball over the creek or down the fairway past the rough. We try to keep in mind that it is only a game of not to take it too serious. But as competitors it is hard to laugh it off hole after hole when we are not playing well.

Most of each hole at our little course has its know little problems. Tight fairway, sand trap in front of the green, or creek to hit over. I am sure that many other golf courses across the country or for that matter around the world has the same situation. But we like to think ours is different.

Chapter 9

The Eyes Have It

When this group first started out most could see the golf ball they hit down the fairway or on the green. As the years went on that became a problem. First you would hear after the golfer swung "where did it go". Reason he kept his head down. Not really. He would swing so hard that he head was all over the place and that the ball maybe traveled 20 yards or went flying to the right or hooked to the left.

That was the start of where did it go. The eyes of many of the W.A.G.A. golfers started to go the way of the old folks. Many times the golfer would think he could see his where he hit his ball. The most common thought was that he hit a lot further than the ball really traveled.

90% of the time the ball traveled only about 50 % of the distance.

I must say now, that most of the guys who realize that their eyes are not what they use to be will ask "did you see my shot" or "where did go". There are a few that claim to see where their ball has gone but what can I tell you, their ball did not go where he claimed to have gone.

A see an eye dog could do better than some of us claim to do.

Now there have been a few who have had their cataract removed. They claim they can really been able to see that little golf ball a good distance down the fairway. Well, we can talk about that in great details and write another book and how I can see the ball down the fairway.

Am sure as the years go on, there will be a need for more help to follow the ball after we hit of the ball. Hopefully, we will be able to follow the ball as we put.

Chapter 10

Travel Day

About four to five times this group would travel to other golf courses. This would happen when for some reason the time we would like to play on our course it was not available. Some other event would be schedule. So we would put up a sign up sheet in the locker room for all those who would like to play another course. Teams would be picked a few days in advance and the fee per player would be increased to $10 per player.

Many of us would looked forward to playing other courses. We would travel anywhere from 20 to 30 miles away. One time we did do an overnight. We stayed in an old motel that had a lot of Peacock on the grounds. They are a pretty bird, but they also make a lot of racket during the night that kept over half of up most of the night. This was the only over night outing for the group. It didn't help the golfers the next morning.

Chapter 11

As the years gone on, every ones handicap starts to go north just like the ages of the W.A.G.A. golfer. With that happening, rules had to be changed. It was decided that if you are a certain age and your handicap has gone north you can move up from the blue tees to the whites. This made many of golfer very happy. It must be said that some of those who move up were doing very well in collecting the winnings after the golf game. You would be surprise how happy some of the W/A.G.A. like to see their handicap go up. They enjoy the extra yards they get and can sore more points.

Also, a few of the golfers who have gotten up in age and as their handicap has escalated they hit from the gold tees. I guess you call them the golden age players. You like to have them on your team because on a good day for one of them they can score a lot of points as they would get two strokes on every hole, including the par Three's.

It won't be long before more and more of the group will be playing from different tees.

Chapter 12

There are time on the golf course that you always take course for granted. When you have played it for so many years you never think that things have changed.

There was a time and this a true story. One late summer day a foursome playing on the back nine had tee off and were walking down the fairway talking about the days events. Not paying to much attentions as to where their ball had landed. As they were approaching the middle of the fairway they started to point out who's ball belong to who. I guess they were not paying to much attention. One by one each golfer approaches their ball and proceeded to their second shot. The last to hit. His ball in deep grass. The golfer gave a strong swing. At impact the supposed ball broke into a million pieces.

Well, to every ones amazement they could not believe their eyes. They called out, what was that. So after a few minutes they realized that what the golfer thought was a golf ball was nothing but a mushroom.

Now, talk about being old and not seeing things as they are, this one takes the cake. Walking up to what you think is a golf ball but in real life is a mushroom and hitting it. I wonder if the rules on golf has a chapter covering this type of situation. I doubt it. Maybe it should be ruled on and written in the rules of golf. "When mistakenly hitting a mushroom on the fairway thinking the ball was yours, there is a two stroke plenty" I think that is fair enough. If anyone has any other ruling please let us know.

Chapter 13

Now there is golfers who spend a lot of time looking for golf balls in tall grass or in creeks or ponds along the fairways. Those are the golfers who brag that they never have had to buy a golf ball ever. I have met a few of them. they spend as much time finding golf balls then playing golf.

A few have found themselves in trouble. Then on a occasion who could hear two golfers debating who saw a loss ball first.

One day a golf ball hawker saw a few golf balls on a creek. He jump put his cart with a retriever and started down the slopped. He had a miss step and ended in the creek. He got the loss balls and also got soak and wet just for a golf ball At the next get together he was awarded a certificate for bravery plus a pair of water goggles, so if happen again he could go deeper in the water to find more golf balls. True story.

Chapter 14

See Eye Golfer

So many times when your near the green you take your putter and wedge to chip up on the green. While you putt you leave your wedge on the side of the green. Now a normal person would remember to pick it up as he leaves. Our guys are not normal golfers. On one occasion we played three holes when one of the guys could not find his wedge. He looked and looked thru his bag. He couldn't fine it. He got back in the golf cart and headed back to the holes he played. Three holes back with no luck he looked in his golf bag again and discovered the club was not in his bag but in his partner's bag who he share the cart with. Now granted our eye sight is not the greatest, but this what happens when get to our age and can't see the club until it hits you in the head. Now the other three gofers had to wait for the missing club golfer. The three who waited had a few choice words for the missed place club player. That's why we our part of the W.A.G.A. group.

Chapter 15

Lost Club

One of the great stories was how one of them lost a golf club on a par three hole.

After the golfer hit the ball and the three others watch the flight of the ball which landed on the green, the golfer who hit the ball looked around and asked the guys in his group if anyone saw where his golf club went. Well, they looked all over and no one could fine the club.

Well, a couple weeks later a different foursome were on that same tee. One golfer happen to looked up in the tree for no reason and spotted a club nested in the tree. That was the same club that they could not fine a few weeks back.

Now, how can something like that happen. You hit the ball and lose the grip and the club ends up in the tree. The club was nested in the tree was about a good twenty feet above ground.

Chapter 16

You wonder sometimes where these golfer get their equipment. A few have got a mix bag of clubs that they purchased over the years.

And some have old tees and old golf balls they happen to fine in the garage. While playing a different course one golfer got up to the tee and put his ball on the tee. Took his normal warm up and then step up to the ball and gave it good whack. Low and behold as the ball traveled thru the air it became two balls. The ball split in two. One part landed on the green. The other in the ruff off the green. His fellow golfer where in amazement. They couldn't believe what they had just seen. They asked where in the hell did you get that ball.

His answer was I found them in the garage this

morning. They have been' there a few years. They were ancient. I believe it was a PoDo golf ball.

Now the question which half of the ball do you play? He played the one on the green and would you believe he claims he made a par.

We never got a ruling on this.

Chapter 17

Never Bought a New Golf Ball

Thru the years there are players who's biggest joy on the golf course is to find lost golf balls. player couldn't walk by a creek or high grass without looking for golf balls. There was one I knew that did that every round. On many golf courses on the edge of the course where homes were owners would have a little stand selling golf balls that landed in thrive yard. This one person who would walk the creeks and high greens looking for golf balls would stop by now many occasions to buy a couple. To find out when he passed away he had a large garbage can in his garage filled golf balls. There are few who I met to claim to never purchase a golf ball in all the years in playing golf.

Chapter 18

New Rules Of Golf For Seniors

Well this group is still active today and play every Tuesday and Thursday at the same time. There are a few less players today, Plus many new faces. The stories are the same today as they were years ago.

A few years ago some one put together new golf rulings for those who were over the age of 70. Some are kind of interesting. Well, interesting if you are not keeping score and are out there just to enjoy the day. Plus have a good beer after a day on the course.

Here they are:

Also good reading.

The Best Damn Golf Book....Period

Chapter 1. How to Properly Line up Your Fourth Putt

Chapter 2 How to Hit a Nikeform the Rough When You Hit a Titleist from the Tee.

Chapter 3 How to avoid the water When you lie 8 in a Bunker

Chapter 4 How to get More Distance Off at the Shank

Chapter 5 When to give the Ranger the finger.

Chapter 6 Using your shadow the Green Maximize Earnings

Chapter 7 Crying and How to handle it.

Chapter 8 How to Rationalize a 6 hour round

Chapter 9 How to find a ball that everyone else saw it go into the water

Chapter 10 How to relax when your hitting Three off the tee

Chapter 11 When to regret your ball Retriever.

Summary

In the beginning, some thirty years ago there was just a foursome that played every Tuesday and Thursday. I had just retired and loved to play golf. I knew one of the original players and he invited me to play with group. They had a few others at that time so now there were two foursomes. The next year more retired guys who loved to play golf join up. So it grew and grew. Along the way, someone had mentioned that we should have a name for this group. In joking someone came up with the name. We voted on it and it became the official name:

Summary

In the begining, some thirty years ago there was just a foursome that played every Tuesday and Thursday.I had just retired and loved to play golf.
I knew one of the original players and he invited me to play with group. They had a few others at that time so now there were two foursomes.The next year more retired guys who loved to play golf join up. So it grew and grew.

Along the way some one had mentioned that we should have a name for this group. In joking some one came up with the name. We voted on it and it became the official name:

W.A.G.A.

That's an abbreiation as the real full name is :

Wrinkle

Ass

Golf

Association